TESSA DISTOR

ECONOMIC UNCERTAINTY

Real Estate Is A Refuge

First edition

This book was professionally typeset on Reedsy.
Find out more at reedsy.com

"Real estate is not just a roof over our heads, but a sanctuary for our dreams."

-TESSA DISTOR (AUTHOR)

Contents

DEDICATION

To my life, Rica,

You are the light that shines bright in my life every single day. You are the reason I wake up each morning with a smile on my face and the reason I keep pushing through even when times get tough. Your love and support mean everything to me, and I am so grateful for the privilege of being your mom. Thank you for bringing so much joy and love into my life.

To my husband, Ricky,

You are my rock, my best friend, and my soulmate. Your unwavering love and support have been my constant source of strength and inspiration. You have been my partner through thick and thin, and I am forever grateful for your presence.

To my Mommy and Daddy,

You have always been my support pillars, role models, and inspiration. You have nurtured, encouraged, and believed in me every step of the way. I am who I am today because of your unwavering love, guidance, and support. Thank you for always being there for my greatest cheerleader and me.

To my dear siblings John, Melissa, and Patricia,

You have been my lifelong companions, confidantes, and best friends. You have always been there for me through thick and thin, and I cannot imagine my life without you. Thank you for being my constant source of love, support, and inspiration.

To my dear Jax and Bella,

You are not just pets; you are part of our family. Your unconditional love, loyalty, and companionship have brought me joy and happiness. Thank you for your wagging tails, wet noses, and endless cuddles. You bring me comfort, laughter, and love daily, and I am grateful for every moment I spend with you.

To all of you,

You are my why. I am forever grateful for having you all in my life. Thank you for being my greatest blessings, family, home, and furry friends, Jax and Bella.

INTRODUCTION

Economic uncertainty is an inevitable part of the financial world, with fluctuations in the market affecting various sectors, including real estate. During such uncertain times, it is essential to have a comprehensive understanding of the real estate market and its relationship with inflation.

In the book "**Economic Uncertainty: Real Estate Is A Refuge,**" we explore the effects of inflation on the real estate market and offer strategies to take advantage of these fluctuations to maximize profitability. This book will provide valuable insights and helpful tips for homeowners, home buyers, and real estate investors.

Chapter 1: Understanding Inflation

Inflation is the rate at which the general price level of goods and services increases over time. Understanding the types of inflation, measuring inflation, and its impact on the world economy is critical in comprehending how it affects the real estate market. For example, during high inflation, real estate can serve as a hedge against the rising cost of living. As inflation increases, the value of real estate assets also tends to appreciate, making it an attractive investment opportunity.

Chapter 2: Real Estate Market

The real estate market encompasses all activities involved in buying, selling, renting, and financing real estate. Understanding the types of real estate, factors affecting the real estate market, and trends in the market is crucial in identifying profitable investment opportunities. For instance, during economic uncertainty, home buyers can take advantage of lower prices in the real estate market to purchase homes that may have been unaffordable during stable economic times.

Chapter 3: Real Estate and Inflation

Inflation significantly impacts the real estate market, affecting property values and the rental market. Real estate investors can take advantage of inflation by investing in properties with the potential for rental income. For example, landlords can increase rent to keep up with inflation, ensuring a steady flow of income. Understanding how inflation affects the rental market can help landlords develop helpful tips to manage their properties and increase profitability.

Chapter 4: Historical Analysis of Real Estate and Inflation

A historic real estate and inflation analysis offer valuable insights into how past experiences can inform future investment decisions. For instance, understanding how the real estate market performed during inflationary periods can help investors identify trends and develop risk management strategies to maximize profits.

Chapter 5: Strategies for Real Estate Investment in Inflationary Periods

Investors can take advantage of inflationary periods by diversifying their portfolios and investing in alternative real estate options such as real estate investment trusts (REITs). Diversification ensures investors spread risk across different investment opportunities, minimizing losses during economic uncertainties.

Chapter 6: Government Policies and Inflation

Government policies play a significant role in the real estate market, affecting financing options, mortgage rates, and other aspects of real estate investment. Understanding how government policies impact the real estate market can help investors develop effective strategies to maximize profitability.

Chapter 7: Real Estate Market Outlook

Predictions for the future real estate market during inflationary periods offer valuable insights into the opportunities and challenges that lie ahead. By understanding the effects of inflation on the future real estate market, investors can develop strategies to take advantage of opportunities and overcome challenges to maximize profits.

In conclusion, **"Economic Uncertainty: Real Estate Is A Refuge"** is a comprehensive guide that offers valuable insights and strategies for homeowners, home buyers, and real estate investors during economic uncertainty. By understanding how inflation affects the real estate market and developing effective risk management strategies, investors can take advantage of opportunities to maximize profitability. This book is a must-read for anyone interested in real estate investment.

Chapter 1

UNDERSTANDING INFLATION

Inflation is a sustained increase in the general price level of goods and services in an economy over time. It is measured by calculating the percentage change in the consumer price index (CPI) over a specified period. Inflation is an important economic concept because it affects the purchasing power of individuals, the profitability of businesses, and the economy's overall health.

There are several causes of inflation, including demand-pull, cost-push, and monetary.

Demand-pull inflation occurs when there is a high level of demand for goods and services in an economy relative to the supply. This can occur due to many factors, including a growing population, increases in consumer confidence, and changes in government policies that encourage spending. As demand increases, prices rise, leading to inflation.

Cost-push inflation occurs when the cost of production increases, forcing businesses to raise prices to maintain their profit margins. This can happen due to several factors, including increases in the cost of labor, raw materials, or energy. For example, if the price of oil increases, transportation costs rise, and the cost of producing goods and services goes up, leading to higher prices and inflation.

Monetary inflation occurs when there is an increase in the money supply in an economy relative to the collection of goods and services. This can happen due to several factors, including changes in government monetary policies, such as lowering interest rates or increases in government spending. As the money supply increases, the value of each unit of currency decreases, leading to inflation. Several other factors can contribute to inflation, including supply shocks, such as natural disasters or geopolitical events, which disrupt the supply of goods and services, and expectations of future inflation, leading to higher prices as businesses and individuals adjust their behavior to account for future price increases.

Inflation can have both positive and negative effects on an economy. On the positive side, moderate inflation levels can encourage spending and investment, as individuals and businesses are motivated to take advantage of rising prices. In addition, inflation can help to reduce the actual value of debt, making it easier for borrowers to pay off their loans. However, high levels of inflation can be damaging to an economy, leading to decreased purchasing power, reduced economic growth, and increased uncertainty and risk.

Governments and central banks have several tools to manage inflation, including monetary policy tools, such as raising or lowering interest rates, and fiscal policy tools, such as increasing or decreasing government spending. In addition, governments can implement policies to encourage economic growth and productivity, which can help mitigate inflation's adverse effects.

Inflation is a sustained increase in the general price level of goods and services in an economy over time. Several factors, including demand-pull inflation, cost-push inflation, and monetary inflation, can cause it. Inflation can have positive and negative effects on an economy, and governments and central

2

banks have several tools at their disposal to manage inflation and ensure the economy's overall health.

TYPES OF INFLATION

There are several types of inflation and examples, including:

1. Demand-Pull Inflation: This type of inflation occurs when an increase in demand for goods and services exceeds the available supply. As a result, prices rise to balance the supply and demand equation. This type of inflation is often seen during periods of economic growth when consumers and businesses are optimistic about the future and increase their spending. For example, in the 1960s, the US experienced demand-pull inflation due to increased government spending on the Vietnam War and social programs, which increased consumer demand.

2. Cost-Push Inflation: This type of inflation occurs when the cost of production of goods and services increases, leading to higher consumer prices. This can happen due to improved raw materials, labor, or energy costs. For example, in the 1970s, the US experienced cost-push inflation due to rising oil prices caused by the OPEC oil embargo.

3. Built-in Inflation: This type of inflation occurs when inflation becomes embedded in the economy, such that workers demand higher wages, and businesses increase their prices to keep up with the rising cost of living. High inflation levels often cause this type of inflation over an extended period. For example, in the 1970s, inflation in the US became built-in, leading to wage-price spirals that made it difficult to control.

4. Hyperinflation: This high inflation level leads to rapid and out-of-control

price increases. Hyperinflation often occurs during political or economic instability, such as wars or financial crises. For example, in the 1920s, Germany experienced hyperinflation due to the country's war reparations and economic instability, leading to a rapid devaluation of the currency.

5. Deflation: This is the opposite of inflation and occurs when an economy decreases the general price level of goods and services. This can happen due to various factors, such as a decrease in demand or an increase in productivity. Deflation can be harmful to an economy as it can lead to decreased spending, decreased economic growth, and increased debt burdens. For example, Japan experienced deflation in the 1990s and 2000s, contributing to the country's "Lost Decade" of economic stagnation.

Understanding the different types of inflation is essential for policymakers, economists, and investors, as each type of inflation requires different approaches to manage and control it. By identifying the kind of inflation occurring, policymakers can take appropriate actions to stabilize the economy and prevent the negative consequences of inflation.

MEASURING INFLATION

Inflation is a crucial measure of economic performance and is closely monitored by policymakers, investors, and businesses. Inflation is the rate at which the general level of prices for goods and services is rising, and it can significantly impact the economy as a whole. To measure inflation accurately, economists use a variety of methods and indicators. In this book, we will explore how economists measure inflation and the different tools and techniques they use.

1. CONSUMER PRICE INDEX (CPI)

One of the most widely used measures of inflation is the Consumer Price Index (CPI). The CPI measures the average price change of a basket of household goods and services. The CPI is calculated by collecting price data for various goods and services, including food, housing, transportation, and medical care. Then, these prices are weighted based on their importance in the average household's budget.

The CPI is calculated by the Bureau of Labor Statistics (BLS), a government agency responsible for collecting and analyzing data on economic activity in the United States. The BLS collects monthly price data for a representative sample of goods and services from thousands of nationwide retail establishments. The CPI is calculated by comparing the cost of the basket of goods and services in the current period to the cost of the same basket of goods and services in a base period. The CPI is a valuable tool for measuring inflation because it reflects consumers' prices for goods and services. However, the CPI has some limitations. For example, the CPI does not account for changes in consumer behavior in response to price changes. If the price of a particular item rises, consumers may substitute a different, lower-priced item, which could affect the overall inflation rate.

2. PRODUCER PRICE INDEX (PPI)

Another measure of inflation is the Producer Price Index (PPI). The PPI measures the average price change domestic producers receive for their goods and services. The PPI is calculated by collecting price data for various goods and services businesses produce, including raw materials, intermediate goods, and finished goods.

The BLS calculates the PPI using data collected from a sample of businesses nationwide. The PPI is useful for measuring inflation at the producer level and can provide insights into the cost pressures that companies face.

3. GROSS DOMESTIC PRODUCT (GDP) DEFLATOR

The Gross Domestic Product (GDP) deflator is another measure of inflation that economists use. The GDP deflator measures the price change of all goods and services produced in an economy. It is calculated by dividing the nominal GDP (the value of all goods and services produced at current prices) by the real GDP (the value of all goods and services produced in an economy at constant prices).

The GDP deflator helps measure inflation at the national level and can provide insights into the economy's overall performance. However, the GDP deflator has some limitations. For example, it may not capture price changes for specific goods and services or reflect changes in consumer behavior.

4. PERSONAL CONSUMPTION EXPENDITURES (PCE) PRICE INDEX

The Personal Consumption Expenditures (PCE) Price Index is another measure of inflation that economists use. The PCE Price Index is similar to the CPI but includes a broader range of goods and services and uses a different weighting system.

The PCE Price Index is calculated by the Bureau of Economic Analysis (BEA), a government agency responsible for collecting and analyzing data on economic activity in the United States. The PCE Price Index is useful for measuring inflation at the consumer level and can provide insights into changes in consumer behavior and spending patterns.

5. WAGE AND SALARY DATA CAN ALSO BE USED TO MEASURE INFLATION.

As the cost-of-living increases, workers may demand higher wages to maintain their standard of living. This can lead to a wage-price spiral, where rising wages lead to higher prices and higher wage demands. There are several ways to measure wage and salary inflation:

5.1. AVERAGE HOURLY EARNINGS

The Average Hourly Earnings (AHE) measure tracks changes in the average hourly wage for non-farm workers in the US. This data is collected by the Bureau of Labor Statistics (BLS) and released monthly. AHE measures the hourly earnings of production and non-supervisory workers in the private sector. It is considered a leading indicator of inflation, as rising wages may lead to higher prices.

5.2. EMPLOYMENT COST INDEX

The Employment Cost Index (ECI) measures changes in the cost of labor for businesses. It includes wages, salaries, and benefits such as health insurance and retirement plans. The ECI is released quarterly by the BLS and is considered a broader measure of labor costs than the AHE. Increases in the ECI can lead to higher prices for goods and services as businesses may pass on the higher costs to consumers.

5.3. UNIT LABOR COSTS

Unit Labor Costs (ULC) measure the labor cost per output unit. It is calculated by dividing total labor costs by total output. ULC is an essential measure of inflation, as rising labor costs can lead to higher prices for goods and services. It is also considered a leading indicator of inflation, as businesses may adjust prices in response to changes in labor costs.

5.4. NATIONAL COMPENSATION SURVEY

The National Compensation Survey (NCS) is conducted by the BLS and provides data on employer-provided compensation, including wages, salaries, and benefits. The NCS covers various industries and occupations and is released annually. The data can be used to track changes in labor costs over time and provide insights into wage and salary inflation trends.

Wage and salary data can be used to measure inflation by tracking changes in the cost of labor for businesses and workers. Increases in wages and salaries can lead to higher prices for goods and services and be a leading indicator of inflation.

These measures of inflation can be used to track price level changes over time and compare inflation rates across different countries or regions. Policymakers and economists use this information to make decisions about monetary policy, fiscal mommy yes policy, and other economic policies that can impact the inflation rate.

EFFECTS OF INFLATION ON THE WORLD ECONOMY

Inflation is a common phenomenon in economies around the world. It occurs when the overall price level of goods and services in an economy increases over time. While moderate inflation can stimulate economic growth, high or persistent inflation can seriously affect the world economy. In this book, we will discuss the various effects of inflation on the world economy.

1. REDUCED PURCHASING POWER

One of the most apparent effects of inflation is reduced purchasing power. Inflation causes the cost of goods and services to increase, which means that consumers can buy fewer goods and services with the same amount of money. This can lead to decreased demand for goods and services, slowing economic growth.

For example, if a loaf of bread costs $4 today and inflation causes the price to increase to $4.40 next year, consumers can buy less bread with the same amount of money. This means they will have less disposable income to spend on other goods and services, which can reduce demand and harm the economy.

2. INCREASED PRODUCTION COSTS

Inflation can also increase production costs for businesses. As labor and raw materials increase, companies must spend more money to produce goods and services. This can lead to higher prices for goods and services, reducing demand and hurting the economy.

For example, if inflation causes the cost of steel to increase, a car manufacturer will need to spend more money to purchase steel to produce cars. This will increase the cost of production, which will be passed on to consumers in the form of higher car prices. As a result, consumers may choose to delay purchasing a car, which can reduce car demand and harm the economy.

3. DECREASED SAVINGS

Inflation can also decrease the value of savings. As the cost of living increases, the purchasing power of savings decreases. This can discourage people from saving money, as they may feel their savings are losing value. This can make it difficult for individuals to plan for the future and reduce overall economic stability.

For example, if inflation is high, an individual who saves $100 may find that their savings have decreased by 5% due to inflation. This means their salvation can buy fewer goods and services than before, discouraging saving and reducing overall economic stability.

4. INCREASED INTEREST RATES

Inflation can lead to an increase in interest rates. As inflation increases, central banks may attempt to control inflation by raising the cost of borrowing. This can make it more expensive for businesses and individuals to borrow money, slowing economic growth.

For example, if inflation is high, the central bank may increase interest rates to reduce the money available for borrowing. This can increase the cost of borrowing for businesses and individuals, reducing investment and harming the economy.

5. DECREASED INVESTMENT

Inflation can also decrease investment. Investors may hesitate to invest in an uncertain economic environment, which can reduce the amount of money available for investment. This can lead to a decrease in job creation and economic growth.

For example, if inflation is high, investors may hesitate to invest in businesses or projects negatively affected by inflation. This can reduce the amount of money available for investment, harming economic growth.

6. REDISTRIBUTION OF WEALTH

Redistribution of wealth can occur as a result of inflation. When the rate of inflation increases, the purchasing power of money decreases, which means that the value of assets and investments denominated in that currency also decreases. This can lead to a transfer of wealth from lenders to borrowers, as borrowers who have borrowed money at a fixed interest rate will be able to repay their debts with money that has less purchasing power.

For example, suppose an individual borrows $10,000 at a fixed interest rate of 5% for five years. After two years, the inflation rate increases from 2% to 5%. This means that the dollar's purchasing power has decreased by 3%. At the end of the five-year term, the individual must repay the loan with $11,628, assuming the interest rate remains fixed. However, due to the increased inflation, the $11,628 the individual repays will have less purchasing power than the $10,000 they borrowed.

In this example, the borrower benefits from the decrease in purchasing power of money, as they can repay their debt with money that has less value. However, the lender needs help, as they receive money back with less purchasing power than when they lent it. This can lead to a transfer of wealth from lenders to borrowers, leading to economic instability.

Redistribution of wealth can also occur due to inflation if wages and salaries do not keep up with the inflation rate. In this case, workers' purchasing power decreases, while the owners of capital benefit from the increased value of their assets. This can exacerbate income inequality and lead to social and political unrest.

Inflation can have significant effects on the world economy. High inflation can reduce purchasing power, increase production costs, decrease savings, increase interest rates, decrease investment, and redistribute wealth. It is essential for governments and central banks to monitor inflation and take action to maintain economic stability.

Chapter 2

REAL ESTATE MARKET

DEFINITION OF REAL ESTATE MARKET

The real estate market is a complex and dynamic economic marketplace where buyers and sellers of real estate assets interact to conduct transactions. It is a critical component of the economy and plays an essential role in providing shelter, commercial space, and infrastructure to support economic activity. Real estate assets include physical properties such as residential, commercial, industrial, and agricultural properties, intangible assets such as real estate investment trusts (REITs), and other financial instruments used to invest in the real estate sector.

Many factors, including economic conditions, government policies, demographics, social trends, and technological advancements, influence the real estate market. These factors impact the demand and supply of real estate assets and determine the price and quantity of assets traded in the market.

Population growth is one of the primary factors driving demand in the real estate market. As populations grow, there is a greater demand for housing and commercial space. Migration patterns also influence demand as people move to different areas for work, education, or lifestyle. Job creation is another significant demand driver, as new jobs require new offices and industrial spaces. Finally, urbanization significantly impacts the demand for real estate assets as people move from rural areas to urban centers.

The supply of real estate assets is influenced by several factors, including zoning regulations, construction costs, availability of land, and environmental restrictions. Zoning regulations dictate the permitted use and density of properties in different areas, which can significantly impact the supply of real estate assets in those areas. Construction costs include the costs of labor, materials, and land and can impact the supply of new developments in the market. The availability of land also influences the collection of real estate assets, as areas with limited land availability may experience higher property prices due to scarcity. Finally, environmental restrictions such as protected wetlands, endangered species habitats, and other factors can limit the availability of land for development and, in turn, impact the supply of real estate assets.

Real estate market transactions involve a significant amount of money. Market participants are exposed to various risks, such as market volatility, liquidity, interest rate, and credit risk. Different financial instruments, such as mortgage-backed securities (MBS), collateralized debt obligations (CDOs), and real estate derivatives, have been developed to mitigate these risks.

A pool of mortgages backs mortgage-backed securities (MBS), and the cash flows from these mortgages are used to pay interest and principal on the deposits. Government agencies such as Fannie Mae and Freddie Mac or private financial institutions can issue mortgage-backed securities.

Collateralized debt obligations (CDOs) are securities backed by a pool of debt instruments, such as mortgages, bonds, and loans. The cash flows from these debt instruments are used to pay interest and principal on the securities. Investment banks or other financial institutions can issue CDOs.

Real estate derivatives are financial instruments that allow investors to speculate on the future price of real estate assets or hedge against price changes. Real estate derivatives can take many forms, including futures contracts, options, and swaps.

The real estate market is a critical component of the economy and has far-reaching implications for individuals and the broader economy. The real estate market's performance can impact household wealth, consumer spending, and employment, among other factors. Therefore, understanding the real estate market and its drivers is essential for policymakers, investors, and individuals alike.

TYPES OF REAL ESTATE

Real estate is a diverse asset class that includes various property types, each with unique characteristics and investment potential. Here are some of the most common types of real estate around the world:

1. Residential Real Estate: This includes single-family homes, multi-family homes, townhouses, and apartments. Residential real estate is typically used for living purposes and is the most common type.

2. Commercial Real Estate: This includes office buildings, retail spaces, shopping centers, hotels, and warehouses. Commercial real estate is used for business purposes and is an essential component of the economy.

3. Industrial Real Estate includes factories, warehouses, and distribution centers. Industrial real estate is used for manufacturing, storage, and distribution purposes and is crucial for the supply chain.

4. Agricultural Real Estate includes farmland, ranches, and orchards.

Agricultural real estate is used for farming and agricultural purposes.

5. Special Purpose Real Estate: This includes properties designed for a specific use, such as hospitals, universities, and religious institutions.

6. Mixed-Use Real Estate: This includes properties that have a combination of residential, commercial, and industrial uses. Mixed-use real estate can consist of apartments with retail on the ground floor, office buildings with apartments on the upper floors, or industrial parks with office spaces.

7. Real Estate Investment Trusts (REITs): REITs are publicly traded companies that own and operate income-producing real estate assets. REITs allow individual investors to invest in a diversified portfolio of real estate assets without purchasing the properties themselves.

In addition to these types of real estate, there are different investment strategies and approaches to real estate investing, including value, growth, income, and development. Each approach has unique characteristics and risks, and investors should carefully consider their investment goals and risk tolerance when selecting a real estate investment strategy.

FACTORS AFFECTING THE REAL ESTATE MARKET

The real estate market is a complex ecosystem that is influenced by a variety of factors. The most significant factors affecting the real estate market include economic conditions, demographics, government policies, interest rates, and technological advancements.

This book will explore these factors in more detail and provide examples of how they can impact the real estate market.

1. ECONOMIC CONDITIONS:

The performance of the overall economy can significantly impact the real estate market. When the economy is thriving, employment rates are high, and consumers have more disposable income, which can drive up demand for real estate. Conversely, when the economy is struggling, unemployment rates increase, and consumer spending decreases, which can lead to a decrease in demand for real estate.

For example, during the Great Recession of 2008, the housing market crashed due to economic factors, including high unemployment rates, a subprime mortgage crisis, and a decline in consumer confidence. As a result, home values plummeted, and millions of homeowners were forced into foreclosure. However, as the economy began to recover, the real estate market bounced back, and home values rose again.

2. DEMOGRAPHICS:

Changes in population demographics can also significantly impact the real estate market. As populations age and new generations enter the housing market, demand for different types of properties can shift. For example, as the baby boomer generation begins to retire, they may be more likely to downsize their homes, which can increase demand for smaller properties. Conversely, as younger generations enter the workforce, they may be more likely to rent or purchase condos or townhouses, increasing demand for these properties.

In addition to changes in age demographics, other demographic factors can also impact the real estate market. For example, changes in immigration policies or trends can influence demand for certain types of properties in specific geographic areas.

3. GOVERNMENT POLICIES:

Government policies can significantly impact the real estate market. Policies related to taxation, zoning, and land-use regulations can all influence the supply and demand of real estate. For example, tax incentives for homeownership can increase demand for real estate, while zoning regulations that restrict development in certain areas can limit real estate supply.

Changes in government policies related to lending and finance can also significantly impact the real estate market. For example, changes in interest rates or mortgage lending standards can affect the affordability of homes, which can impact demand.

4. INTEREST RATES:

Interest rates can have a significant impact on the real estate market. When interest rates are low, borrowing costs are reduced, which can lead to increased demand for real estate. Conversely, when interest rates are high, borrowing costs increase, which can decrease demand for real estate.

For example, in the years following the Great Recession, the Federal Reserve lowered interest rates to historic lows to stimulate the economy. These low rates led to a surge in demand for real estate as homebuyers were able to take advantage of more affordable borrowing costs.

5. TECHNOLOGICAL ADVANCEMENTS:

Technological advancements are changing the real estate market in significant ways. The rise of online real estate platforms and virtual reality technology has made it easier for buyers and sellers to connect, view properties, and complete transactions remotely. In addition, advances in energy-efficient building materials and innovative home technology are changing how properties are designed and built.

For example, the COVID-19 pandemic has accelerated the adoption of remote work, which has led to increased demand for properties with home office spaces and outdoor amenities. Additionally, the rise of sustainable building practices and innovative home technology influences the properties being developed and the features buyers are looking for.

Various factors, including economic conditions, demographics, government policies, interest rates, and technological advancement, influence the real estate market.

TRENDS IN THE REAL ESTATE MARKET

The real estate market is constantly changing, influenced by various factors, including economic conditions, demographics, technology, and social trends. Understanding these trends is crucial for investors and consumers, as it can provide insight into where the market is heading and what areas may offer the most growth potential.

Several key trends have emerged in the real estate market in recent years, shaping the industry and driving new developments. Here are some of the most notable trends in the real estate market today:

1. Urbanization: One of the most significant trends in the real estate market is urbanization, with more and more people moving into cities. This trend has been fueled by various factors, including job opportunities, better access to education and healthcare, and a desire for a more active lifestyle. As a result, urban areas have become hotbeds for new developments, with many cities experiencing a surge in construction activity.

2. Affordable housing: With urbanization comes a growing need for affordable housing. Many people move to cities for job opportunities but face high housing costs. This has created a demand for affordable housing, leading to new developments and creative solutions, such as micro-housing and co-living spaces.

3. Sustainability: Another trend in the real estate market is a growing focus on sustainability. This includes using renewable energy sources, such as solar and wind power, and incorporating green building practices, such as LEED certification. Developers also incorporate sustainable materials and designs into their buildings, creating eco-friendly living spaces.

4. Technology: The real estate industry has been transformed by technol-

ogy, with new tools and platforms making it easier to buy, sell, and manage properties. For example, virtual reality technology creates immersive experiences for buyers, allowing them to tour properties virtually before purchasing. Blockchain technology is also being used to streamline the buying and selling process, making it more secure and efficient.

5. Aging population: As the population ages, there is a growing demand for senior living communities and assisted living facilities. This has created opportunities for developers to create specialized housing options for seniors, including active adult communities and memory care facilities.

6. Co-working spaces: The rise of the gig economy has led to a growing demand for co-working spaces, with more and more people working remotely or as independent contractors. This has created opportunities for developers to create shared workspaces with amenities like high-speed internet, meeting rooms, and networking opportunities.

7. Retail: The retail industry has undergone a significant transformation, with many traditional brick-and-mortar stores needing help to compete with online retailers. This has created opportunities for developers to repurpose vacant retail spaces, transforming them into mixed-use developments incorporating residential, office, and retail spaces.

8. Smart homes: Another trend in the real estate market is the rise of smart homes, which incorporate advanced technology such as home automation systems, voice-controlled assistants, and smart thermostats. This has created opportunities for developers to build energy-efficient homes and offers a high level of convenience and customization for homeowners.

9. Short-term rentals: The rise of short-term rental platforms such as Airbnb has created new opportunities for investors and property owners. Many are now investing in properties, specifically for short-term rentals, creating a new type of real estate investment.

10. International investment: Finally, the real estate market is increasingly global, with investors seeking opportunities in new markets worldwide. This has led to a surge in international investment, with many developers

and investors looking to tap into new markets and take advantage of emerging trends.

The real estate market is constantly evolving and adapting to new trends and developments, influenced by various factors such as technology, demographics, economics, and societal changes. These trends can significantly impact the industry, shaping how properties are bought, sold, and managed.

One of the most significant trends in recent years has been the rise of technology in the real estate industry. With the advent of online marketplaces and virtual tours, buyers and sellers are no longer limited to in-person interactions. This has made it easier for people to buy and sell properties from anywhere in the world, increasing the competition for properties and driving up prices in some areas.

Another trend in the real estate market is the focus on sustainability and eco-friendliness. As more people become aware of the impact of climate change, they are increasingly looking for energy-efficient properties built using sustainable materials. This has led to a rise in demand for green buildings and homes and the development of new technologies, such as solar panels and innovative home systems.

The rise of co-living and co-working spaces is another trend that has gained traction in recent years. With the increased remote work and the sharing economy, people seek flexible, community-oriented living and working spaces. Co-living spaces offer shared living areas and amenities, while co-working spaces provide shared office spaces and resources. These spaces are trendy among younger generations, who value experiences and community over material possessions.

In addition, the real estate market has seen a rise in demand for luxury properties and amenities, particularly in urban areas. High-end apartments and condos with amenities like rooftop pools, fitness centers, and concierge services are becoming more common in cities worldwide. These properties are often marketed to high-net-worth individuals and cater to a luxurious lifestyle.

Finally, the real estate market is also influenced by demographic shifts, particularly by the aging population. As more baby boomers reach retirement age, there is a growing demand for senior living facilities and retirement communities. These properties offer specialized amenities and services for older adults, including medical care, meal plans, and social activities.

The real estate market is constantly evolving and adapting to new trends and developments, driven by various factors such as technology, sustainability, community, luxury, and demographics. These trends significantly impact the industry, shaping how properties are bought, sold, and managed. As the world continues to change, it will be interesting to see how the real estate market continues to evolve and adapt to new challenges and opportunities.

Chapter 3

REAL ESTATE AND INFLATION

HOW INFLATION AFFECTS THE REAL ESTATE MARKET

I nflation can have a significant impact on the real estate market around the world. The effects of inflation can be positive or negative, depending on various factors such as the level and speed of inflation, the economic conditions of a country, and the characteristics of the real estate market. This book will discuss how inflation affects the real estate market worldwide.

1. Buyers' purchasing power: Inflation can affect buyers' purchasing power, as the value of money decreases over time due to inflation. This means that buyers have to pay more to purchase the same property, as real estate prices also increase due to inflation. This can decrease demand for real estate, as buyers may be reluctant to invest in properties that have increased in value beyond their budget.

2. Interest rates: Inflation can increase as central banks raise rates to control inflation. This can significantly impact the real estate market, as higher

interest rates make it more expensive for buyers to borrow money to purchase properties. This can lead to decreased demand for real estate, as buyers may need more money to afford higher mortgage payments.

3. Construction costs: Inflation can also affect the construction costs of real estate projects, as the prices of materials, labor, and other inputs increase due to inflation. This can decrease the supply of new properties, as developers may need help to build new projects. This can lead to a shortage of properties, which can increase prices and lead to a seller's market.

4. Rental rates: Inflation can also affect rental rates, as landlords may increase rents to cover the increased costs of maintaining and managing properties. This can decrease demand for rental properties, as tenants may need help to afford higher rents. This can also lead to a reduction in the value of rental properties, as the income generated by these properties may decrease due to the decline in demand.

5. Investment potential: Inflation can also affect the investment potential of real estate properties, as the value of assets increases over time due to inflation. This means that real estate can serve as a hedge against inflation, as the value of properties increases along with the inflation rate. This can make real estate an attractive investment option for those looking to protect their wealth from the effects of inflation.

6. Global economic conditions: Inflation can also be influenced by global economic conditions, such as the currency's value, international trade agreements, and geopolitical tensions. This can significantly impact the real estate market, as investors may be more or less willing to invest in properties based on the economic conditions of a country. For example, if a country experiences high inflation and economic instability, investors may be hesitant to invest in real estate in that country.

Inflation can have a significant impact on the real estate market around the world. The effects of inflation can be positive and negative, depending on various factors such as the level and speed of inflation, the economic conditions of a country, and the characteristics of the real estate market. Real estate investors and professionals should be aware of the potential effects of inflation on the market and adapt their strategies accordingly.

EFFECTS OF INFLATION ON PROPERTY VALUES

Real estate and inflation are two interconnected concepts critical to the global economy. Real estate refers to the land and buildings used for residential, commercial, industrial, and other purposes. Conversely, inflation refers to the general increase in the price of goods and services in an economy over time. In this book, we will define real estate and inflation, explore their relationship, and discuss the implications of inflation on the real estate market.

Real estate is a broad term that encompasses land and any buildings or structures attached to it. It includes residential properties, such as single-family homes, apartments, and condominiums, and commercial properties, such as office buildings, retail spaces, and warehouses. Industrial properties, such as factories and manufacturing plants, are also included in the real estate market. Real estate can also have undeveloped land or land with improvements, such as landscaping and infrastructure.

Real estate is a critical component of the economy and contributes to employment, income, and economic growth. Various factors influence the real estate market, including interest rates, supply and demand, consumer behavior, government policies, and economic conditions.

Inflation is the general increase in the price of goods and services in an economy over time. When inflation occurs, the purchasing power of a currency decreases, and consumers can buy fewer goods and services with the same amount of money. Inflation is measured using an inflation index, such as the Consumer Price Index (CPI), which tracks the prices of a basket of goods and services over time. Inflation can have a range of impacts on the economy, including reducing the value of savings, increasing the cost of borrowing, and affecting consumer behavior. High inflation levels can lead to economic instability and negatively impact employment and economic growth.

Inflation can have significant implications for the real estate market. Some of the importance of inflation on the real estate market include:

1. IMPACT ON HOUSING AFFORDABILITY

Inflation can reduce housing affordability as building materials and labor costs increase. This can make it more challenging for consumers to access affordable housing, particularly for low-income families. Policymakers and real estate investors may need to prioritize affordable housing projects to ensure access to housing for all.

2. IMPACT ON INTEREST RATES

Inflation can lead to higher interest rates, increasing borrowing costs for consumers and businesses. This can reduce demand for real estate and lead to lower prices. Real estate continues investors may need to consider the impact of interest rates on their investments and adjust their strategies accordingly.

3. IMPACT ON REAL ESTATE INVESTMENTS

Inflation can impact the value of real estate investments. Real estate assets may be viewed as an inflation hedge, as the asset's value may increase during inflationary periods. However, higher inflation can also lead to higher property taxes and maintenance costs, reducing the profitability of real estate investments.

4. IMPACT ON COMMERCIAL REAL ESTATE

Inflation can impact the commercial real estate market, particularly regarding lease agreements. Lease agreements may include inflation clauses that adjust rent prices based on changes in the CPI or other inflation indices. Inflation can also impact the demand for commercial real estate, as businesses may reduce their expenses during inflationary periods.

5. IMPACT ON THE CONSTRUCTION INDUSTRY

Inflation can increase the cost of building materials and labor, impacting the construction industry. Higher construction costs can reduce the supply of new real estate, leading to higher prices for existing properties. The construction industry may need to adjust its pricing strategies during inflationary periods to remain competitive.

Real estate and inflation are critical interconnected concepts that significantly impact the economy. Real estate is a broad term that encompasses land and buildings used for residential, commercial, industrial, and other purposes. Inflation refers to the general increase in the price of goods and services in an economy over time.

Inflation can impact the real estate market in various ways, including interest rates, supply and demand, and consumer behavior. Real estate investments can also impact inflation through the construction industry, contributing to the economy's production of goods and services.

The implications of inflation on the real estate market include impacts on housing affordability, interest rates, real estate investments, commercial real estate, and the construction industry. Policymakers and real estate investors need to consider the impacts of inflation on the real estate market and adjust their strategies accordingly.

Overall, the relationship between real estate and inflation is complex and requires a nuanced understanding of the factors influencing both concepts. By understanding the relationship between real estate and inflation, economists, investors, and policymakers can make informed decisions that support economic growth and stability.

Inflation can significantly impact property values and the overall real estate market. As inflation increases, the cost of goods and services rises, and the purchasing power of money decreases. This means the same amount of money will buy fewer goods and services, including real estate. Here are some of the effects of inflation on property values and how the market is reacting to these changes:

1. Increased property values: One of the ways inflations can affect real estate is by increasing property values. As the cost of goods and services rises, the value of real estate may also increase, especially in areas with high demand for property. This is because investors may see real estate as a safer investment option than other assets, such as stocks or bonds, which can be more volatile during inflationary periods.

2. Higher interest rates: Inflation can also lead to higher interest rates, as central banks may increase interest rates to control inflation. Higher interest rates can make it more expensive for individuals and businesses to borrow money, reducing demand for real estate. This can lead to decreased property values, particularly for properties that require financing.

3. Reduced affordability: Inflation can also reduce real estate affordability for buyers. As the cost-of-living increases, buyers may have less money to spend on real estate purchases. This can lead to a decrease in demand for real estate, which can lower property values.

4. Increased construction costs: Inflation can also increase the cost of construction, which can impact property values. As building materials, labor, and other construction-related expenses rise, developers may charge higher prices for new construction projects to make a profit. This can lead to higher home prices, which can impact the affordability of real estate.

In response to these changes, the real estate market may react in different ways depending on the level of inflation and other economic factors. For example, during periods of high inflation, demand for real estate may decrease, leading to lower property values. This can create opportunities for buyers to purchase properties at a lower cost. On the other hand, during periods of low inflation, demand for real estate may increase, leading to higher property values.

Additionally, the market may respond to changes in inflation by adjusting interest rates and lending standards. For example, if interest rates rise due to inflation, lenders may require higher down payments and credit scores for real estate loans, making it more difficult for buyers to obtain financing.

Inflation can significantly impact property values and the overall real estate market. It can lead to higher property values, reduced affordability, higher construction costs, and changes in interest rates and lending standards. The market may respond to these changes by adjusting demand, pricing, and financing options. Understanding the relationship between inflation and real estate is crucial for buyers, sellers, and investors to make informed market decisions.

RENTAL MARKET AND INFLATION

The rental market is one of the critical sectors of the real estate industry, and it is also significantly influenced by inflation. Inflation affects rental markets differently, and understanding the relationship between the two is essential for landlords. In this section, we will discuss the effects of inflation on rental needs and provide helpful tips for landlords.

EFFECTS OF INFLATION ON THE RENTAL MARKET

1. Increase in Rent Prices: Inflation often increases rent prices. This is because landlords have to pay more for their expenses, such as utilities, property taxes, and maintenance costs. To maintain their profit margins, landlords increase the rent prices to offset their increased expenses.
2. Decrease in Vacancy Rates: Inflation can decrease vacancy rates in rental markets. This is because when inflation is high, the cost-of-living increases and people may have difficulty affording a down payment for a home. As a result, more people tend to rent, leading to a decrease in vacancy rates.
3. Increase in Property Values: Inflation can increase property values, affecting rental markets. Higher property values mean landlords can charge higher rents, increasing competition among renters.
4. Increase in Operating Costs: Inflation leads to an increase in operating costs for landlords. They must pay more for utilities, maintenance, and property taxes. As a result, landlords may have to reduce their profit margins or increase rent prices to offset these costs.

HELPFUL TIPS FOR LANDLORDS

1. Increase rent prices gradually: Landlords should avoid increasing rent prices too quickly, which may drive away tenants. Gradual rent increases are more manageable for tenants and less likely to cause them financial hardship.
2. Monitor the market: Landlords should closely monitor the market trends and adjust their rental prices accordingly. If inflation increases demand for rental properties, landlords can take advantage of the

situation by raising rents.

3. Improve efficiency: Landlords can improve the efficiency of their properties to save on operating costs. This includes upgrading appliances, using energy-efficient lighting and HVAC systems, and investing in water-saving devices.

4. Build good relationships with tenants: Building good relationships with tenants can help landlords retain them for extended periods, reducing vacancy rates. Good relationships can be built by responding promptly to maintenance requests, being respectful, and offering fair rents.

5. Consider offering incentives: Landlords can provide incentives to attract tenants during high inflation. This can include offering a free month's rent, waiving application fees, or providing other incentives that tenants find appealing.

Inflation is a significant factor that can affect the rental market. It can lead to an increase in rent prices, a decrease in vacancy rates, and an increase in operating costs for landlords. However, landlords can mitigate inflation's effects by increasing rent prices gradually, monitoring the rental market, improving efficiency, building good relationships with tenants, and offering incentives. By following these tips, landlords can maintain their profitability while providing quality rental properties to tenants.

IMPACT ON MORTGAGE RATES AND FINANCING OPTIONS

Inflation can have a significant impact on mortgage rates and financing options. When inflation increases, it often leads to higher interest rates, affecting existing and new mortgages. This, in turn, can make it harder for homebuyers to qualify for mortgages and afford homes, as higher interest rates increase the cost of borrowing money.

One way that inflation can impact mortgage rates is through the central bank's actions. To combat inflation, central banks may raise interest rates, which can increase the cost of borrowing money for banks and lenders. As a result, lenders may pass these increased costs onto borrowers through higher mortgage rates.

Another way that inflation can affect mortgage rates is through changes in investor behavior. When inflation rises, investors may demand higher returns on their investments to compensate for the increased risk of inflation eroding their returns. This can lead to higher yields on government bonds, often used as a benchmark for mortgage rates.

Furthermore, inflation can also impact financing options for homebuyers. In a high-inflation environment, lenders may be more cautious about offering adjustable-rate mortgages (ARMs), which have interest rates that fluctuate based on market conditions. This is because inflation can make it difficult to predict future interest rates, and a sudden rise in rates could make it difficult for borrowers to keep up with their payments.

In addition to affecting mortgage rates and financing options, inflation can also impact the housing market. When inflation rises, it can lead to higher construction costs, slowing down new home construction and reducing the supply of homes on the market.

This, in turn, can drive up home prices even further, making it more difficult for homebuyers to afford a home.

To cope with the impact of inflation on mortgage rates and financing options, homeowners and homebuyers can take several steps. For example, they can consider locking in a fixed-rate mortgage, protecting them from future interest rate increases. They can also shop around for the best mortgage rates and consider alternative financing options, such as FHA or VA loans, which may have more favorable terms.

Homeowners and homebuyers can cope with the impact of inflation on mortgage rates and financing options in several ways:

1. Refinance at a lower rate: Homeowners can refinance their existing mortgages at a lower rate if interest rates have decreased. This can help them save money on their monthly mortgage payments.

2. Consider adjustable-rate mortgages (ARMs): ARMs are mortgage loans with an interest rate that adjusts periodically based on market conditions. They can offer lower initial interest rates than fixed-rate mortgages, making homeownership more affordable. However, homeowners should know their monthly mortgage payments can increase if interest rates rise.

3. Shop for the best rates: Homebuyers can shop for the best mortgage rates and financing options to find the most affordable option. Comparing rates from multiple lenders ensures you get the best deal.

4. Consider a larger down payment: Homebuyers can consider making a larger down payment on their home purchase to reduce the amount of the loan and the resulting interest payments. This can also make them more attractive to lenders and increase the likelihood of being approved for a loan.

5. Seek professional advice: Homeowners and homebuyers can seek the advice of a financial advisor or mortgage broker to help them navigate the impact of inflation on mortgage rates and financing options. These professionals can offer guidance on the best strategies for managing inflation-related risks and finding the most affordable financing options.

Additionally, homeowners can make their homes more energy-efficient, which can help them save money on utilities and reduce their overall housing costs. This can include upgrading insulation, installing energy-efficient appliances, and adding solar panels.

Inflation can have a significant impact on mortgage rates and financing options, as well as the overall housing market. Homeowners and homebuyers should be aware of these impacts and please take steps to mitigate them, such as locking in a fixed-rate mortgage or improving their home's energy efficiency.

Chapter 4

HISTORICAL ANALYSIS OF REAL ESTATE AND INFLATION

H istorically, real estate markets have exhibited different trends during inflationary periods. Inflationary periods are generally characterized by rising prices, higher interest rates, and decreased purchasing power. This can significantly impact the real estate market, closely tied to interest rates and purchasing power.

During periods of high inflation, mortgage interest rates tend to increase, which can lead to a decrease in demand for real estate. Higher interest rates increase the cost of borrowing, making it more difficult for potential homebuyers to afford a mortgage. As a result, home prices may decrease as sellers are forced to lower their costs to attract buyers.

On the other hand, real estate assets can serve as a hedge against inflation. Real estate values tend to increase along with inflation, meaning property owners can benefit from rising prices. This can be particularly true for commercial real estate, as rising prices can lead to higher rents and increased profits for landlords.

Additionally, investors may turn to real estate as a safe-haven investment during inflationary periods. This is because real estate values tend to be more stable than other assets during economic uncertainty, making it a good investment option for those looking to protect their wealth.

One unique example of factors during inflationary periods in the real estate market is the 1970s in the United States. During this time, inflation was high, with consumer prices increasing at an average rate of over 10% per year between 1973 and 1980. As a result, mortgage interest rates rose sharply, reaching a high of over 18% in 1981.

These high-interest rates made it difficult for many Americans to afford homes, leading to decreased demand for real estate. This decrease in demand, coupled with high inflation and the recession of the early 1980s, led to a significant decline in real estate values. By 1982, home prices had fallen by over 20% in many areas, leaving many homeowners underwater on their mortgages.

However, the real estate market eventually recovered from this downturn. In the mid-1980s, interest rates decreased, and the economy improved. This led to increased demand for real estate, and home prices began to rise again.

The historical trends in the real estate market during inflationary periods have been mixed, with both positive and negative effects on the market. However, it is essential to note that every inflationary period is unique. The impact on the real estate market will depend on various factors, including interest rates, economic conditions, and the availability of financing options.

Here are some helpful case studies of the real estate market during inflationary periods:

1. United States, the 1970s: During the 1970s, the United States experienced a period of high inflation, known as the "Great Inflation." During this time,

real estate prices also increased significantly. However, the rise in interest rates led to a decrease in the demand for real estate, and prices began to decline in the early 1980s. This resulted in a period of stagnation in the real estate market, which lasted until the mid-1990s.

2. Germany, 1920s: During the hyperinflation in Germany in the 1920s, real estate prices soared as people sought to invest in tangible assets that would hold their value. However, the value of the German mark was so volatile that real estate prices were often quoted in gold or other foreign currencies. The instability of the money and the economy made it difficult for homeowners to maintain their properties, and many were forced to sell at a loss.

3. Japan, the 1980s: During the 1980s, Japan experienced economic growth and high inflation. Real estate prices increased rapidly, and many people invested heavily in property. However, the market became overheated, and in the early 1990s, a real estate bubble burst. Property values plummeted, leaving many investors with significant losses.

4. Venezuela, the 2010s: Venezuela has experienced hyperinflation since the 2010s, with the inflation rate reaching over 1,000,000% in 2018. As a result, real estate prices have skyrocketed, but currency instability and economic turmoil have made it difficult for people to purchase and maintain properties. Many homeowners have been forced to sell at a loss or abandon their properties altogether.

5. Zimbabwe, the 2000s: During the 2000s, Zimbabwe experienced hyperinflation, with the inflation rate reaching over 79 billion percent in 2008. Real estate prices increased significantly during this time, but the economic instability and political turmoil made it difficult for people to purchase and maintain properties. Many properties were abandoned or destroyed, and the real estate market has not fully recovered.

In general, during inflationary periods, real estate prices tend to increase due to the depreciation of the currency and the desire to invest in tangible assets. However, this price increase may be unsustainable and lead to market bubbles that eventually burst, resulting in significant investor losses. It is essential for investors to carefully evaluate a country's economic and political conditions before investing in real estate during inflationary periods.

LESSONS LEARNED FROM PAST EXPERIENCES

Many countries have experienced periods of high inflation that have significantly impacted their economies and societies. These experiences have taught us several lessons about inflation and how to manage it effectively. Some of these lessons include:

1. Various factors can cause inflation: Inflation can be caused by a range of factors, including government policies such as excessive money printing, supply chain disruptions, geopolitical tensions, and changes in consumer behavior. Understanding the root causes of inflation is crucial for developing effective management strategies.

2. High inflation can have severe economic consequences: High inflation can erode the purchasing power of individuals' savings and wages, leading to a declining standard of living. It can also lead to economic instability, such as increased unemployment, reduced investment, and slowed economic growth.

3. Managing inflation requires a balanced approach: Inflation management requires a delicate balance between controlling prices and maintaining economic growth. Central banks play a critical role in managing inflation by adjusting interest rates, controlling the money supply, and monitoring economic indicators.

4. Real estate is a valuable inflation hedge: It can be an effective hedge against inflation because it tends to appreciate over time. During periods of inflation, real estate prices often increase faster than the general price level, making it an attractive investment option for those seeking to protect their wealth.

5. Policy coordination is essential: Managing inflation effectively requires coordination between various government departments, including the central

bank, finance ministry, and economic planning agencies. Effective communication and collaboration are essential to developing and implementing coordinated policy responses to inflationary pressures.

6. Prevention is better than cure: It is easier to prevent inflation from occurring than to manage it once it has taken hold. Policymakers must adopt a proactive approach to inflation management, addressing potential risks and implementing measures to prevent inflation from spiraling out of control.

The lessons learned from past experiences with inflation demonstrate the importance of effective inflation management and the need for a balanced approach to managing economic growth and price stability. Policymakers must remain vigilant and proactive in monitoring inflationary pressures, developing effective strategies to manage them, and transparently communicating their policies and actions to the public.

Chapter 5

STRATEGIES FOR REAL ESTATE INVESTMENT IN INFLATIONARY PERIODS

DIVERSIFICATION OF PORTFOLIO

D iversifying portfolios is essential for managing risk and achieving long-term financial goals. The basic idea behind diversification is to spread your investments across different asset classes and industries to minimize the impact of any investment's performance on your overall portfolio.

Here are some helpful examples of how to diversify your portfolio:

1. Invest in different asset classes: One of the simplest ways to diversify your portfolio is to invest in different asset classes, such as stocks, bonds, and real estate. Each asset class has its unique risk profile and can perform differently in other market conditions, so spreading your investments across multiple asset classes can help reduce overall portfolio risk.

2. Invest in different industries: Investing in other sectors is another way to diversify your portfolio. For example, if you have a large portion of your portfolio invested in the technology sector, consider adding exposure to

healthcare, energy, or consumer goods to balance your portfolio.

3. Invest in different geographies: Investing in different countries and regions can also help diversify your portfolio. Countries have other economies, political systems, and market conditions, leading to various investment opportunities and risks. For example, investing in emerging markets can provide growth potential but comes with higher risk.

4. Use index funds or ETFs: Index funds and ETFs (exchange-traded funds) are investment vehicles that expose a broad range of assets or markets. Investing in these funds allows you to diversify quickly without selecting individual investments.

5. Consider alternative investments: Alternative investments, such as private equity, hedge funds, and commodities, can also benefit diversification. However, these investments often come with higher fees and liquidity risks, so carefully evaluating the risks and benefits is essential before investing.

It's important to note that diversification does not guarantee profits or protect against losses, and it's essential to review regularly and adjust your portfolio to align with your financial goals and risk tolerance. A financial advisor can also help you develop a customized diversification strategy tailored to your needs and circumstances.

INVESTING IN ALTERNATIVE REAL ESTATE OPTIONS

Investing in alternative real estate options can help to diversify an investor's portfolio and protect against the adverse effects of inflation on the traditional real estate market. Alternative real estate options refer to non-traditional assets that can provide investors with different returns and risk profiles.

One example of an alternative real estate option is investing in real estate investment trusts (REITs), publicly traded companies that own and operate income-producing real estate properties. REITs can allow investors to invest in real estate without direct property ownership. They can offer diversification benefits as they invest in different types of properties across different geographies.

Another alternative real estate option is investing in real estate crowdfunding platforms, which allow investors to invest in real estate projects alongside other investors. This can provide investors access to real estate investments that they might not have been able to access otherwise. It can also offer diversification benefits as investors can invest in multiple projects with smaller amounts of capital.

Investing in agricultural land is another alternative real estate option that can help to protect against inflation. Agricultural land can provide investors with a tangible asset that can appreciate over time and generate income through leasing the land to farmers.

Investing in self-storage facilities is another alternative real estate option providing diversification benefits and protects against inflation. Self-storage facilities can be less vulnerable to economic downturns as they provide a basic need for individuals and businesses to store their possessions.

Diversifying a real estate portfolio by investing in alternative options can help protect against inflation's adverse effects on the traditional real estate market. By investing in various assets with different risk profiles and return expectations, investors can reduce their exposure to any asset class and create a more resilient portfolio.

INVESTING IN REAL ESTATE INVESTMENT TRUSTS (REITS)

Real estate investment trusts (REITs) are investment vehicles that allow individuals to invest in a diversified pool of income-producing real estate assets. These assets may include commercial properties such as shopping malls, office buildings, and hotels and residential properties such as apartments and single-family homes.

Investing in REITs can be a great way to gain exposure to the real estate market without purchasing and managing properties directly. Here are some steps to consider when investing in REITs:

1. Research REITs: The first step in investing in REITs is to research the available options. There are different REIT types, such as equity REITs that own and manage properties, mortgage REITs that invest in real estate debt, and hybrid REITs that invest in equity and debt. Understanding the different REIT types and their investment strategies is essential before deciding.

2. Analyze the REIT's financials: Once you have identified a REIT that meets your investment criteria, you should analyze the company's financial statements. This includes reviewing its revenue, net income, cash flow, debt levels, and dividend history. It's vital to assess the REIT's ability to generate income and pay dividends to its shareholders.

3. Assess the REIT's portfolio: You should also assess the REIT's real estate portfolio, including the types of properties it owns, their locations, and their occupancy rates. This can give you an idea of the REIT's exposure to different sectors and regions and its growth potential.

4. Consider the management team: The management team of a REIT plays a crucial role in its success. You should research the experience and track record of the REIT's management team, including their ability to execute the company's investment strategy.

5. Evaluate the risks: Investing in REITs involves certain risks, such as interest rate, credit risk, and liquidity risk. Given your investment goals and risk tolerance, you should evaluate the risks associated with the REIT and assess whether they are acceptable.

6. Monitor your investment: Monitoring your investment regularly is essential once you have invested in a REIT. This includes reviewing the company's financial statements, assessing its portfolio, and staying current on market trends and news.

Investing in REITs can be a great way to gain exposure to the real estate market and diversify your portfolio. However, it's essential to research and assesses the risks before investing.

RISK MANAGEMENT STRATEGIES

Real estate investments can be risky during inflationary periods as property values fluctuate significantly. However, investors can use several risk management strategies to minimize risks and boost the world economy. Here are some helpful tips:

1. Diversify your portfolio: Investing in a variety of different real estate assets, such as commercial properties, residential properties, and REITs, can help to minimize the risks associated with inflation. This will ensure a balanced portfolio that can weather any market fluctuations.

2. Hedge against inflation: Investing in assets likely to increase in value during inflationary periods, such as commodities like gold and silver, can help hedge against inflation. This will ensure that your portfolio remains protected even as inflation rates rise.

3. Keep an eye on interest rates: Interest rates can significantly impact real estate investments, as higher interest rates can lead to higher borrowing costs and lower property values. It's essential to monitor interest rates and adjust your investments accordingly.

4. Focus on cash flow: Inflation can significantly impact rental income, as rental rates may not keep pace with inflation rates. Focusing on properties that generate strong cash flow can help to mitigate this risk and ensure that you continue to generate income even during inflationary periods.

5. Consider investing in emerging markets: Emerging markets can offer significant opportunities for real estate investors, as these markets are often less developed and may be less affected by inflation. Investing in emerging markets can help to diversify your portfolio and provide access to new investment opportunities.

6. Stay informed: Finally, it's essential to stay knowledgeable about market trends, economic conditions, and other factors that can impact real estate investments. This will help you to make informed investment decisions and adjust your portfolio as needed.

Real estate investors can minimize risks and boost the world economy by following these risk management strategies. By investing in a diversified portfolio of real estate assets, hedging against inflation, focusing on cash flow, and staying informed, investors can ensure that their investments remain profitable even during inflationary periods.

Chapter 6

GOVERNMENT POLICIES AND INFLATION

Inflationary periods can significantly impact the overall economy and pose challenges for policymakers. Governments may implement different policies to manage inflation and its economic impact. Some of the government policies that can be implemented during an inflationary period are:

1. Monetary policy: Monetary policy is implemented by a country's central bank to manage the supply of money and credit in the economy. In an inflationary period, the central bank may increase the interest rates to decrease the demand for money, which in turn can reduce the overall inflation rate. On the other hand, if inflation is too low, the central bank may lower interest rates to increase the demand for money and boost inflation.

2. Fiscal policy: Fiscal policy uses government spending and taxation to influence the economy. During an inflationary period, the government may implement policies that decrease government spending or increase taxes to reduce the aggregate demand in the economy. This can lead to a decrease in inflation. However, if inflation is too low, the government may increase spending or lower taxes to boost aggregate demand and increase inflation.

3. Supply-side policies: Supply-side policies aim to increase the supply of goods and services in the economy to meet demand. During an inflationary period, the government may implement policies that increase productivity, such as investing in education and training or reducing regulatory barriers to encourage entrepreneurship and innovation. This can increase the supply of goods and services, which can help reduce inflation.

4. Price controls: Governments may also implement price controls during inflation. Price controls can be in the form of maximum prices, where the government sets a limit on how much a reasonable service can be sold, or minimum prices, where the government sets a minimum wage. Price controls can help keep the prices of goods and services low. Still, they can also lead to shortages and decrease the overall quality of goods and services.

5. Exchange rate policy: Exchange rate policy refers to managing a country's currency exchange rate. During an inflationary period, the government may implement policies that devalue the currency, making exports cheaper and imports more expensive. This can decrease the demand for imports and boost the demand for domestic goods and services, leading to a decrease in inflation.

6. Income policies: Income policies refer to the policies that aim to manage wages and salaries. During an inflationary period, the government may implement policies that control wages and salaries, such as wage freezes or caps. This can help reduce inflation but also lead to decreased employee morale and labor strikes.

Inflationary periods can be challenging for policymakers, and there is no one-size-fits-all solution to managing inflation. Governments must analyze the root causes of inflation and implement appropriate policies. It is important to note that some of these policies may have unintended consequences, and policymakers must carefully consider the potential outcomes before implementing them.

HOW GOVERNMENT POLICIES AFFECT THE REAL ESTATE MARKET

Government policies can significantly impact the real estate market positively and negatively. These policies can include regulations, taxes, subsidies, and other incentives designed to stimulate or control the market. In this book, we will explore how government policies can affect the real estate market and how they can be implemented to achieve different outcomes.

1. INTEREST RATES AND MONETARY POLICY

One of the most significant government policies that can impact the real estate market is monetary policy, which includes setting interest rates and controlling the money supply. Lower interest rates make it easier for borrowers to access credit and increase demand for real estate, which can lead to rising prices. Conversely, higher interest rates can make borrowing more expensive, slowing the real estate market.

2. ZONING AND LAND-USE REGULATIONS

Zoning and land-use regulations are also essential government policies that can impact the real estate market. These policies dictate how the land can be used for residential, commercial, or industrial purposes. They can also restrict the density of development or limit the height of buildings. Zoning and land-use regulations can restrict real estate supply, which can drive up prices in certain areas or encourage development, leading to an oversupply of real estate.

3. TAX POLICIES

Tax policies are another significant factor in the real estate market. Property taxes, for example, can increase real estate costs, while tax incentives can encourage investment in certain areas. Capital gains taxes can also impact real estate investors, as they may affect the decision to buy or sell a property. In addition, the tax code can provide incentives for affordable housing development or green building initiatives.

4. SUBSIDIES AND INCENTIVES

Subsidies and incentives are another way the government can impact the real estate market. These policies can be grants, tax credits, or other financial incentives to encourage development or make real estate more affordable. For example, a government might offer subsidies to developers who build affordable housing, or they might provide tax credits for the installation of renewable energy systems in commercial buildings.

5. HOUSING POLICIES

Housing policies can also impact the real estate market. These policies can include programs designed to increase home ownership, such as low-interest loans or down payment assistance. They can also have rental subsidies, which help low-income individuals afford to house. In addition, housing policies can include regulations designed to protect tenants, such as rent control or eviction protections.

6. INFRASTRUCTURE INVESTMENT

Investment in infrastructure, such as roads, public transportation, and utilities, can also impact the real estate market. When infrastructure is improved, it can increase the value of the real estate in the surrounding area. For example, constructing a new subway line can make commuting more accessible for people to work, making homes in the area more valuable. On the other hand, the need for infrastructure investment can limit the value of real estate in certain areas.

7. ENVIRONMENTAL POLICIES

Environmental policies can also impact the real estate market, particularly in areas with concerns about pollution or climate change. These policies can include regulations designed to limit corrosion, such as restrictions on the use of fossil fuels or rules on emissions from industrial facilities. They can also include incentives for green buildings or the installation of renewable energy systems.

Government policies can have a significant impact on the real estate market. These policies can be designed to stimulate or control the market, encourage development or limit it, or promote specific types of real estate investment. By understanding how government policies impact the real estate market, investors can make more informed decisions and adapt to changing conditions.

EXAMPLES OF GOVERNMENT POLICIES THAT IMPACT THE REAL ESTATE MARKET

Many government policies can impact the real estate market. Here are some examples:

1. Monetary Policy: Monetary policy is set by central banks to manage the supply of money and credit in the economy. Central banks can increase interest rates to curb inflation or lower rates to stimulate economic growth. These policies can impact mortgage rates, affecting the demand for housing and the cost of borrowing for real estate investors.

    2. Fiscal Policy: Fiscal policy uses government spending and taxation to influence the economy. For example, the government may offer tax incentives to encourage real estate investment in certain areas or provide funding for affordable housing programs. These policies can impact the housing demand and financing available for real estate investors.

    3. Zoning and Land Use Policies: Zoning and land use policies regulate how the land can be used and developed. For example, a city may enact zoning laws prohibiting commercial development in residential areas. These policies can impact the value of real estate in certain areas and the types of development allowed.

    4. Environmental Regulations: Environmental regulations can impact real estate development by imposing land use and development restrictions. For

example, wetlands regulations may prohibit development on specific parcels of land. These policies can limit the supply of developable land and impact the value of the existing real estate.

5. Rent Control and Tenant Protection Policies: Rent control and tenant protection policies regulate the relationship between landlords and tenants. For example, a city may enact rent control laws limiting the amount landlords can charge for rent. These policies can impact the profitability of real estate investments and the availability of affordable housing.

6. Building Codes and Safety Standards: Building codes and safety standards regulate the construction and maintenance of buildings. These policies can impact the cost of constructing and maintaining real estate and the safety of occupants.

7. Immigration Policy: Immigration policy can impact the demand for housing and the types of real estate investments that are attractive. For example, an influx of immigrants may increase the need for affordable housing or lead to new commercial development in certain areas.

Government policies can have a significant impact on the real estate market. Real estate investors and professionals must stay updated on policy changes and trends to make informed decisions about investments and development opportunities.

Chapter 7

REAL ESTATE MARKET OUTLOOK

Real estate markets have always been a significant factor in the economy of any country. Real estate can contribute to a country's GDP, employment, and investment. As the real estate market is an essential component of the economy, it significantly impacts consumers' day-to-day lives. With inflationary pressures increasing globally, the real estate market is facing new challenges that require a fresh perspective from economists. This book will discuss the real estate market outlook that economists should focus on to help consumers with their day-to-day lives during an inflationary period.

REAL ESTATE MARKET OUTLOOK DURING INFLATIONARY PERIOD

Inflation is a situation where prices rise and the purchasing power of money decreases. The real estate market is not immune to inflationary pressures and faces many challenges during such periods. During an inflationary period, the cost of building materials, labor, and financing increases, which leads to a rise in the overall cost of real estate projects. Inflationary pressures also affect the demand and supply dynamics of the real estate market.

One of the critical factors that economists should focus on during an inflationary period is the impact of inflation on interest rates. Interest rates significantly impact the real estate market as they affect the demand for housing. During inflationary periods, central banks tend to increase interest rates to combat inflation. As interest rates rise, the cost of borrowing increases, which leads to a decrease in demand for housing. A decrease in demand for housing leads to a reduction in real estate prices. Therefore, economists should focus on how inflationary pressures affect interest rates and how interest rates impact the real estate market.

Another critical factor that economists should focus on during an inflationary period is the impact of inflation on the rental market. Inflationary pressures can increase rental rates as landlords pass on the increased maintenance costs, taxes, and utilities to tenants. An increase in rental rates can strain consumers' day-to-day lives, especially those on a fixed income. Therefore, economists should focus on the impact of inflation on the rental market and how it affects consumers' day-to-day lives.

Economists should also focus on the impact of inflation on the availability of credit in the real estate market. During inflationary periods, lenders tighten credit standards, making it difficult for consumers to obtain financing for real estate projects. A decrease in credit availability can lead to a decline in demand for housing and a reduction in real estate prices. Therefore, economists should focus on the impact of inflation on the availability of credit in the real estate market and how it affects consumers' day-to-day lives.

Finally, economists should focus on the impact of inflation on housing affordability. Inflationary pressures can increase the cost of housing, making it difficult for consumers to afford to buy or rent a home. An increase in the price of accommodation can also lead to a decrease in the quality of life for consumers as they may have to compromise on other essential expenses to afford housing. Therefore, economists should focus on the impact of inflation on housing affordability and how it affects consumers' day-to-day lives.

STRATEGIES FOR CONSUMERS DURING INFLATIONARY PERIOD

Consumers can take specific steps to mitigate the impact of inflationary pressures on their day-to-day lives in the real estate market. One key strategy is shopping around for the best mortgage rates and terms. Consumers should compare the rates and terms various lenders offer and choose the most affordable one. Consumers can also consider refinancing their existing mortgages for lower interest rates.

Another strategy for consumers is to look for affordable housing options. During inflationary periods, housing costs tend to increase, making it difficult for consumers to find affordable housing. Consumers should look for options that fit their budget, such as smaller homes, apartments, or more affordable locations. Consumers can also consider renting instead of buying, as rental rates may be more manageable than mortgage payments during an inflationary period.

Another strategy for consumers is to prioritize their expenses. Consumers should identify their essential expenses, such as housing, food, and healthcare, and prioritize them over non-essential expenses. Consumers can also look for ways to save money on their essential expenses, such as shopping for groceries on sale, using coupons, or negotiating with healthcare providers for lower costs.

Finally, consumers can consider investing in real estate to protect themselves from inflation. Real estate can be a hedge against inflation, as it tends to appreciate over time. Consumers can consider investing in real estate through various options, such as buying rental properties, investing in real estate investment trusts (REITs), or participating in real estate crowdfunding.

In conclusion, the real estate market outlook during an inflationary period is complex, and economists should focus on various factors that can impact consumers' day-to-day lives. Economists should focus on the impact of inflation on interest rates, the rental market, the availability of credit, and housing affordability. Consumers can take specific steps to mitigate the effects of inflationary pressures on their day-to-day lives in the real estate market, such as shopping around for the best mortgage rates and terms, looking for affordable housing options, prioritizing their expenses, and considering investing in real estate. By focusing on these factors and strategies, economists and consumers can navigate the real estate market during an inflationary period and protect themselves from its impact on their day-to-day lives.

PREDICTIONS FOR THE FUTURE REAL ESTATE MARKET

The real estate market is expected to evolve and adapt to changing consumer demands, technological advancements, and global events. While there may be some challenges in the short term, the long-term outlook for the real estate market remains positive.

There are some general predictions and trends that may impact the future of the real estate market based on available information and past patterns.

1. Continued demand for housing: The need for housing will likely continue due to population growth, urbanization, and household formation. As a result, the demand for housing will continue to outpace the supply, leading to rising prices in many markets.

2. Technological advancements: Technology is expected to impact the real estate industry significantly. Emerging technologies such as blockchain, virtual reality, and artificial intelligence are expected to streamline processes, enhance customer experiences, and increase transparency in the market.

3. Shift towards sustainability: There is a growing trend towards sustainable building practices and eco-friendly materials. This shift is driven by consumer demand and government regulations, and it will likely continue in the future.

4. Increased affordability challenges: Despite the high housing demand, many consumers face affordability challenges due to rising prices and stagnant wages. This trend is expected to continue, especially in areas with high demand and limited supply.

5. Increased use of data and analytics: real estate companies increasingly use data and analytics to make informed decisions about property investments, market trends, and consumer behavior. This trend is expected to continue, leading to more efficient and accurate decision-making processes.

6. The impact of global events: The real estate market is also likely to be impacted by international events such as political instability, natural disasters, and economic fluctuations. These events can affect the market unpredictably and may lead to changes in investment patterns and consumer behavior.

EFFECTS OF INFLATION ON THE FUTURE REAL ESTATE MARKET

Inflation is a phenomenon marked by a sustained increase in the general price level of an economy's goods and services over time. Various factors, such as an increased money supply, rising production costs, and changes in consumer behavior, cause it. Inflation significantly impacts the economy, and the real estate market is no exception. We will discuss the effects of inflation on the future real estate market in detail.

Inflation can have a significant impact on the real estate market. Inflation can lead to an increase in property prices, higher interest rates, a shift in consumer behavior, an effect on commercial real estate, an impact on REITs, an impact on construction and development, an impact on property taxes, an impact on international real estate investment, and an impact on the mortgage market. It is crucial for real estate investors, developers, and consumers to monitor inflation trends and adjust their strategies accordingly to minimize the impact of inflation on their investments and purchasing decisions.

1. INCREASE IN INTEREST RATES

Inflation can increase interest rates, impacting the real estate market in several ways. When inflation rises, central banks may raise interest rates to control it. Higher interest rates make borrowing more expensive, which can reduce the demand for real estate. This can decrease property prices, especially in markets with weak demand.

Higher interest rates can also impact the affordability of mortgages, making it harder for potential buyers to purchase a property. This can lead to a slowdown in the real estate market as buyers are discouraged from entering the market. However, higher interest rates can also benefit the real estate market by making investments in real estate more attractive than other asset classes, such as bonds and stocks.

2. INCREASE IN PROPERTY PRICES

Inflation can increase property prices as building materials and labor costs increase. This can make it more expensive to build new properties, leading to a decrease in the supply of new homes. At the same time, the demand for housing may remain strong due to population growth, urbanization, and household formation. This can lead to a situation where demand outstrips supply, leading to an increase in property prices.

However, the increase in property prices may not be uniform across all real estate market segments. For example, luxury properties may see a more significant cost increase than affordable housing due to differences in demand and supply dynamics.

3. THE SHIFT IN CONSUMER BEHAVIOR

Inflation can also shift consumer behavior, as consumers may prioritize assets that appreciate over time, such as real estate. This can lead to increased demand for real estate as consumers seek ways to protect their wealth from inflation. This can lead to a situation where demand outstrips supply, leading to an increase in property prices.

However, consumer behavior may also shift towards renting instead of buying, as rising property prices may make it harder for consumers to afford a mortgage. This can increase demand for rental properties, leading to higher rental rates.

4. IMPACT ON COMMERCIAL REAL ESTATE

Inflation can also impact the commercial real estate market, as businesses may face higher operating costs due to rising rents, labor costs, and other expenses. This can lead to companies being more selective in choosing their locations and opting for smaller spaces or places outside prime areas to reduce costs.

Inflation can also impact the value of commercial properties, primarily if the property is leased out to tenants on long-term leases. Inflation can erode the value of fixed rental income over time, decreasing the property's value.

5. IMPACT ON REAL ESTATE INVESTMENT TRUSTS (REITS)

Inflation can impact real estate investment trusts (REITs), publicly traded companies that invest in real estate assets. REITs may face challenges in a high-inflation environment as they may face higher borrowing costs and may be required to pay out higher dividends to investors.

However, REITs can also benefit from inflation as they may own assets that appreciate over time, such as real estate properties. This can lead to an increase in the value of the REIT's portfolio, leading to higher returns for investors.

6. IMPACT ON CONSTRUCTION AND DEVELOPMENT

Inflation can also impact the construction and development of real estate projects. Rising material and labor costs can increase the cost of construction, making it more expensive to build new properties. This can lead to a decrease in the supply of new homes and rising property prices.

Inflation can also impact the profitability of real estate developers and contractors, as rising costs may squeeze their profit margins. This can lead to decreased development of real estate projects, as developers may delay or cancel projects due to lower expected returns.

7. IMPACT ON PROPERTY TAXES

Inflation can also impact property taxes, as local governments may increase property taxes to offset the rising costs of providing public services. This can lead to an increase in the price of owning real estate, reducing the affordability of real estate for some buyers. Property taxes may also impact the profitability of real estate investments, as higher property taxes can reduce the net income generated from rental income.

8. IMPACT ON INTERNATIONAL REAL ESTATE INVESTMENT

Inflation can also impact international real estate investment, as investors may shift their investments to countries with lower inflation rates. This can lead to decreased demand for real estate in high-inflation countries and decreased property prices. However, some investors may view real estate investments in high-inflation countries as a hedge against inflation, as real estate values may appreciate faster than inflation.

9. IMPACT ON THE MORTGAGE MARKET

Inflation can impact the mortgage market in several ways. Rising interest rates can make it more expensive for borrowers to finance their mortgages, reducing the affordability of real estate. Higher inflation rates can also lead to higher mortgage rates, as lenders may increase their interest rates to offset the risk of inflation eroding the loan's value.

Inflation can also impact the availability of mortgage financing, as lenders may become more cautious about lending during periods of high inflation. This can reduce the number of potential buyers in the real estate market, leading to a slowdown.

OPPORTUNITIES AND CHALLENGES IN THE REAL ESTATE MARKET

Opportunities and challenges in the real estate market are constantly evolving and can vary depending on economic conditions, demographics, government regulations, and technology. Here are some of the key opportunities and challenges currently facing the real estate market:

OPPORTUNITIES

1. Low-Interest Rates: Low-interest rates allow homebuyers to obtain mortgages at lower rates, reducing the overall cost of homeownership. This can lead to increased demand for real estate and a potential appreciation in property values.

2. Demographic Shifts: The aging of the baby boomer generation and the rise of millennials as the largest homebuying demographic provide opportunities for real estate investors and developers. Aging baby boomers may look to downsize or move to more urban areas, while millennials may seek affordable housing options in urban centers.

3. Technology: Technology is changing how people search for and buy real estate. Online listings, virtual tours, and digital marketing provide real estate professionals new tools to reach potential buyers and investors. Real estate technology companies are also developing new tools for property management, tenant screening, and property valuation.

4. Sustainability: The growing focus on sustainability and environmentally friendly practices provides opportunities for real estate investors and developers to differentiate their properties and appeal to socially conscious consumers. Green building practices, energy-efficient appliances, and renewable energy systems can also provide cost savings for property owners.

CHALLENGES

1. Affordability: The rising cost of real estate in many urban centers is challenging for many homebuyers and renters, particularly those with lower incomes. This can lead to a need for more affordable housing and the displacement of long-term residents.

2. Economic Uncertainty: Economic uncertainty, such as recessions or market volatility, can impact the real estate market by reducing demand for real estate and making it more difficult for investors to obtain financing.

3. Regulation: Government regulations, such as zoning laws, building codes,

and environmental regulations, can impact the development and profitability of real estate projects. Changes in regulations can also affect the value of existing properties.

4. Competition: The real estate market is highly competitive, with many investors and developers vying for the same properties and tenants. This can lead to increased prices and reduced profitability for some investors.

5. Technology Disruption: While technology provides opportunities for real estate professionals, it can disrupt traditional business models. Online real estate platforms may reduce the need for conventional real estate agents and brokerages.

The real estate market presents opportunities and challenges for investors, developers, and consumers. The key to success in the market is to stay informed about industry trends and adapt to changing market conditions.

Conclusion

RECAP OF KEY POINTS

To recap, some of the key points we have discussed in this book include:

- Real estate is an important asset class that can provide investors with stable returns and diversification benefits.
- Inflation can impact the real estate market by affecting property prices, interest rates, and affordability.
- Real estate investments, particularly those in high-inflation countries or areas with rapidly rising property prices, may offer potential opportunities for investors seeking to hedge against inflation.
- Real estate developers and investors should monitor inflation trends and adjust their strategies accordingly to minimize the impact of inflation on their investments and purchasing decisions.
- Government policies, such as zoning laws and development regulations, can impact the real estate market by affecting the supply of affordable housing and the profitability of real estate projects.

FINAL THOUGHTS ON REAL ESTATE AND INFLATION

Real estate and inflation are complex concepts that are intertwined and have significant impacts on the economy. Real estate is a critical component of the economy and impacts many industries, including construction, finance, and consumer goods. On the other hand, inflation impacts consumers' purchasing power and can affect economic growth and stability.

Real estate investments can provide a hedge against inflation, as the value of real estate assets can appreciate during inflationary periods. However, inflation can also impact the demand for real estate and increase the cost of maintaining and managing real estate assets.

To navigate the impacts of inflation on the real estate market, policymakers and investors must consider various factors, including interest rates, supply and demand, consumer behavior, and construction costs. They must also consider the impact of inflation on multiple sectors of the economy and adjust their strategies accordingly.

Real estate and inflation are complex topics requiring a nuanced understanding of the factors influencing them. By considering the impacts of inflation on the real estate market, policymakers and investors can make informed decisions supporting economic growth and stability while promoting housing affordability and accessibility for consumers.

FUTURE IMPLICATIONS FOR INVESTORS AND POLICYMAKERS

The relationship between real estate and inflation will continue to be essential for policymakers and investors to monitor in the years ahead. As the economy continues to recover from the impacts of the COVID-19 pandemic, inflation is likely to remain a significant consideration for the real estate market.

One implication for investors is that they may need to adjust their strategies to account for the impacts of inflation on real estate investments. For example, rising inflation may lead to higher interest rates, impacting mortgage rates and reducing home demand. Investors may need to consider alternative investments, such as real estate investment trusts (REITs), which are less affected by inflation.

Another implication for investors is that they may need to consider the impact of inflation on construction costs. During inflationary periods, construction materials and labor costs can increase, impacting the profitability of real estate development projects. Investors may need to adjust their expectations for returns on development projects or consider alternative investment opportunities.

For policymakers, managing inflationary pressures while promoting afford-able housing is critical. Policies that promote housing affordability, such as subsidies for low-income housing or incentives for developers to build affordable homes, can help address housing shortages and support economic growth. However, policymakers must also consider the impact of these policies on inflationary pressures and balance the needs of consumers and developers.

Policymakers may also need to consider policies that support the construction industry during inflationary periods. For example, policies that reduce regulatory barriers to construction or provide incentives for construction firms to invest in new technology can help offset the impact of inflation on construction costs.

The relationship between real estate and inflation will continue to be an essential consideration for policymakers and investors in the years ahead. By carefully monitoring inflationary pressures and adjusting policies and investment strategies accordingly, policymakers and investors can support economic growth and stability while promoting housing affordability and accessibility for consumers.

In conclusion, **"Economic Uncertainty: Real Estate Is A Refuge"** by **TESSA**

DISTOR provides a comprehensive analysis of the impact of inflation on the real estate market and offers valuable insights and strategies for investors seeking to navigate economic uncertainty.

The book covers a wide range of topics, from understanding inflation and its effects on the global economy to the various factors affecting the real estate market and historical trends in the industry. The author also offers practical advice for real estate investors, including diversification of portfolios, investing in alternative real estate options, and risk management strategies.

One of the key takeaways from the book is the importance of understanding how inflation affects the real estate market, particularly in terms of property values and rental needs. Real estate investors can benefit from this knowledge by adopting a long-term investment strategy to acquire high-quality properties in areas with strong rental demand.

Moreover, the book highlights the impact of government policies on the real estate market and how policymakers can influence inflation and other economic factors that affect the industry. Investors should stay informed on these policies and their potential impact on the real estate market.

In summary, **"Economic Uncertainty: Real Estate Is A Refuge"** is a valuable resource for investors seeking to navigate economic uncertainty, particularly in inflationary periods. By understanding the unique characteristics of the real estate market and adopting a long-term investment strategy that considers inflation and government policies, investors can benefit from real estate's stability and wealth-generation potential.

Epilogue

How to get rich during economic uncertainty?

Inflation can erode your money's purchasing power, making it difficult to build wealth over time. However, there are some strategies you can use to get rich during inflation potentially:

1. Invest in Real Estate: Real estate can be a good investment option during inflationary periods, as property values tend to increase with inflation. Investing in rental properties or real estate investment trusts (REITs) can provide a steady stream of rental income and long-term capital appreciation.

2. Invest in Stocks: Stocks can be a good hedge against inflation, as the prices of stocks tend to rise with inflation. Investing in stocks that are likely to benefit from inflation, such as companies that produce essential goods or services, can help protect your portfolio from the effects of inflation.

3. Invest in Commodities: Commodities such as gold, silver, and oil are often seen as a hedge against inflation, as their prices tend to increase with inflation. Investing in commodities through exchange-traded funds (ETFs) or mutual funds can help protect your portfolio from inflation.

4. Start a Business: Starting a business can be an excellent way to generate income and build wealth during inflation. You can earn a high return on investment by creating a company that produces goods or services in demand during inflationary periods.

5. Invest in Yourself: During inflation, investing in yourself by developing new skills or pursuing additional education or training can be essential. You can increase your earning potential and build wealth over time by improving your skills and knowledge.

It is important to note that these strategies involve some level of risk. Conducting research and consulting with a financial professional before making investment decisions is essential. Additionally, it is vital to maintain a diversified portfolio and avoid putting all your eggs in one basket.

As I conclude the book **Economic Uncertainty: Real Estate Is A Refuge**, it is essential to remember that economic uncertainty and inflationary periods can significantly impact the real estate market. Homeowners, home buyers, and real estate investors can take advantage of the information shared in this book to navigate through such periods successfully.

For homeowners, it is advisable to maintain and improve the value of their homes during economic uncertainty. This includes keeping up with necessary maintenance, making home improvements to increase the home's value, and having a solid plan to manage unexpected expenses. It is also essential for homeowners to stay informed about government policies that could impact their mortgages and seek professional advice if needed.

For home buyers, it is crucial to be aware of the impact of inflation on mortgage rates and financing options. During periods of high inflation, mortgage rates tend to rise, making it more difficult for home buyers to obtain financing. However, home buyers can use alternative financing options, such as adjustable-rate mortgages or creative financing, to secure a home loan during inflationary periods.

For real estate investors, diversification of their portfolio is critical. They should invest in various properties and consider alternative real estate options, such as commercial and industrial properties, to minimize risk during economic uncertainty. Investing in real estate investment trusts (REITs) can also be a good option for investors, as they provide exposure to real estate while offering liquidity and diversification.

As we look to the future, we must note that the real estate market will face challenges and opportunities. While inflation may threaten property values and rental rates, there is also potential for growth and investment.

In conclusion, I urge you to use the information in this book to make informed decisions about your real estate investments and to stay informed about changes in the market. Doing so allows you to position yourself for success and weather any economic uncertainty.

Thank you for reading "ECONOMIC UNCERTAINTY: Real Estate Is A Refuge," I wish you all the best in your real estate endeavors.

About the Author

With a passion for all things real estate and finance, *Tessa* has helped countless happy homeowners, home buyers, investors, and other professionals navigate complex financial transactions and negotiate favorable deals, selecting the correct solutions and strategies that fit their needs and budget and, in the process, helping them get the home of their dreams, scale their real estate portfolio, and protect their financial assets.

Tessa's keen eye for investments and skills to spot trends and opportunities in the market have earned her a reputation in investment analysis, property valuation, and mortgage financing. She's now on a mission to help people avoid costly mistakes, eliminating any uncertainty related to investment decisions so they can achieve their long-term financial goals.

Having extensive experience in real estate and finance, Tessa has become a highly analytical and detail-oriented professional. She enjoys utilizing her expertise to assist people in all types of negotiations.

She enjoys listening to music, reading a good book, traveling, and hanging out with friends and family when she is not busy.

You can connect with me on:

- http://www.tessadistor.com
- https://twitter.com/411_agency
- https://www.facebook.com/RealEstateWithTessa